Easy

SPANISH

Crossword Puzzles

Stanley Appelbaum and
Nina Barbaresi

DOVER PUBLICATIONS, INC.

New York

Easy Spanish Crossword Puzzles is a new work, first published by
Dover Publications, Inc., in 1993.

International Standard Book Number: 0-486-27452-7

Manufactured in the United States of America
Dover Publications, Inc., 31 East 2nd Street, Mineola, N.Y. 11501

Note

The Spanish names of six familiar things fit into each of the 25 puzzles in this book. The spaces for the words run across and down, and many words cross over each other, sharing letters. To solve each crossword, simply spell out the names of the things shown beneath the puzzle and on the opposite page. The numbers next to each picture show you where the words belong. To help you get started, a few letters have been given in each puzzle. You can check your work by turning to the Solutions that begin on page 54.

On pages 61–64, an alphabetical list is provided of all 150 Spanish words used in the book along with their English equivalents and gender-indicating definite articles (English "the"). The abbreviation FEM. (feminine) has been used with feminine nouns that take the masculine article *el*.

[4]

5

1

4

6

[5]

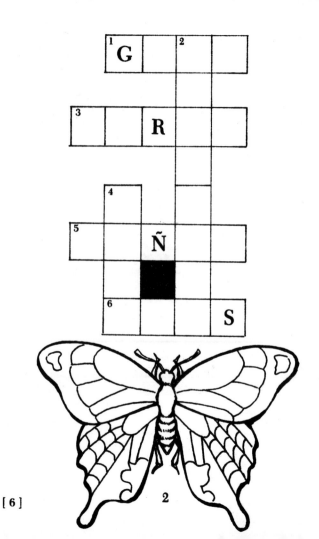

2

4

5

3

1

6

[7]

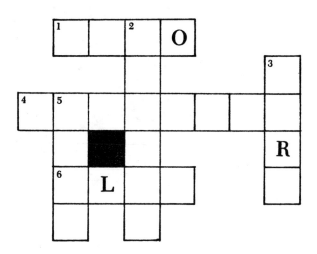

[8]

2

3

5

4

6

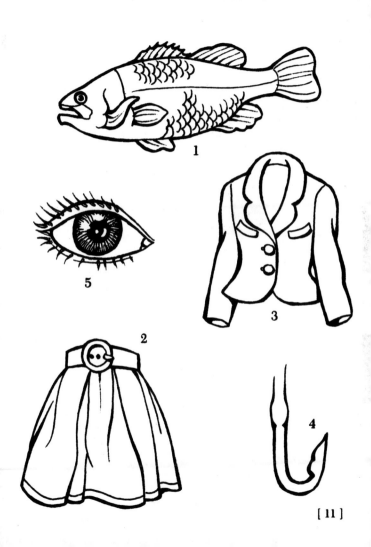

5

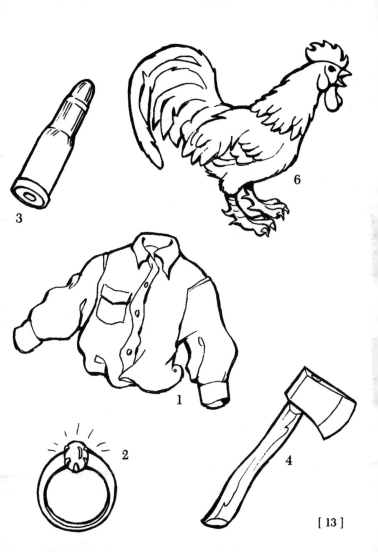

3

6

1

2

4

4

3

2

6

5

3

2

4

5

6

1

6

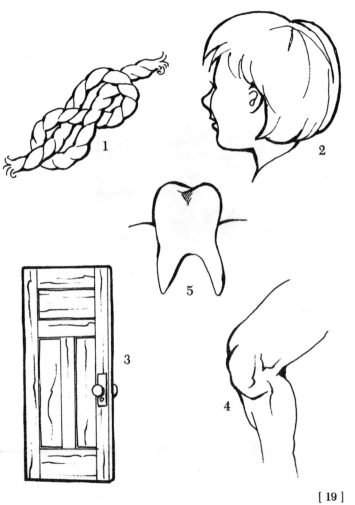

1

2

3

5

4

3

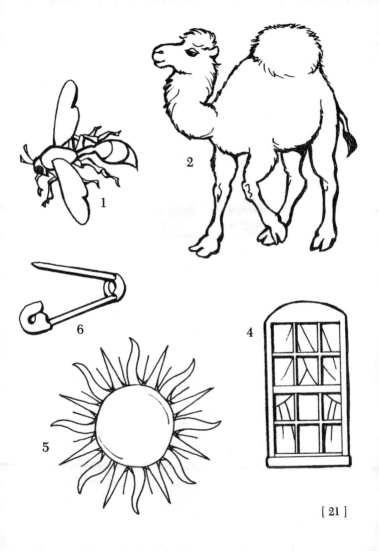

2

4

5

3

6

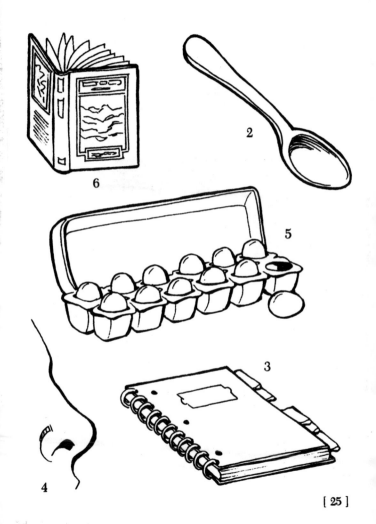

6

2

5

4

3

5

3

6

1

2

4

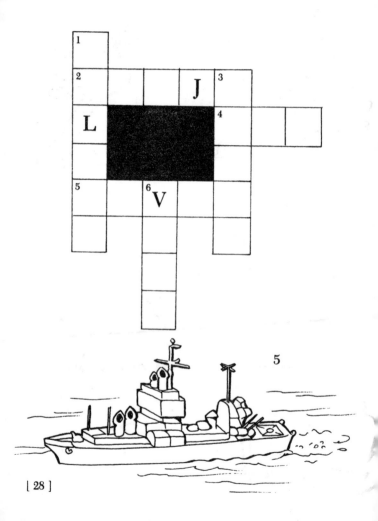

5

3

2

6

4

1

3

4

1

5

6

4

1

3

6

5

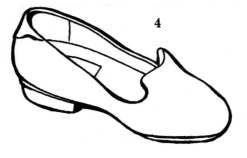

4

6

3

1

5

2

[36]

1

2

6

4

5

6

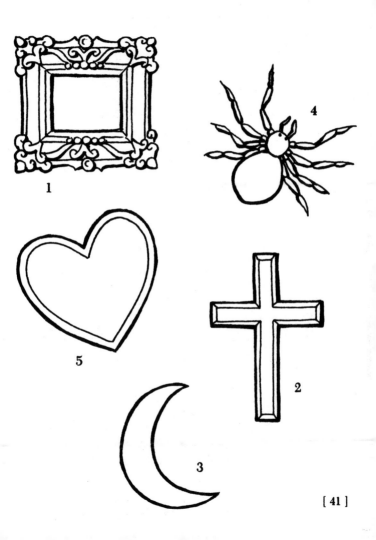

1

4

5

2

3

1

6

2

5

4

3

6

1

5

2

S

L

U

E

3

6

1

2

5

4

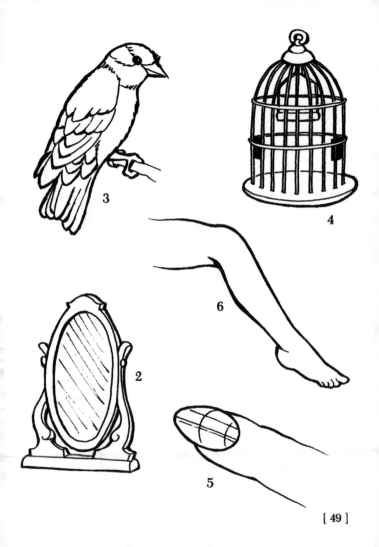

3

4

6

2

5

3

1

2

5

4

6

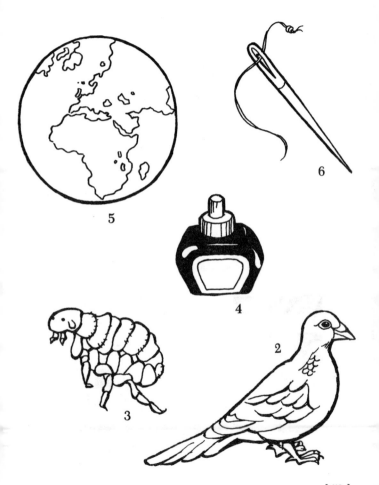

5

6

4

3

2

Solutions

page 4

page 6

page 8

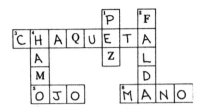

page 10

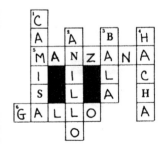

page 12

page 14

page 16

page 18

page 20

page 22

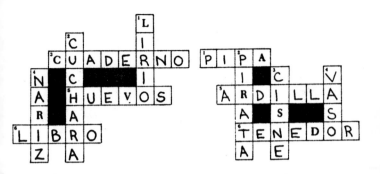

page 24

page 26

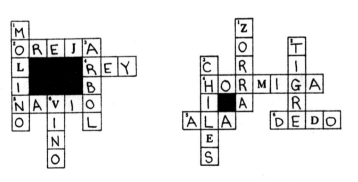

page 28

page 30

page 32

page 34

page 36

page 38

page 40

page 42

page 44

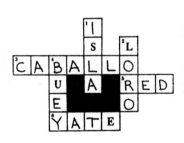

page 46

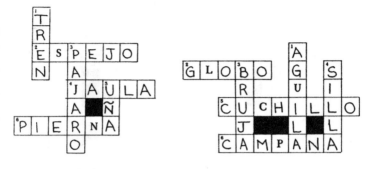

page 48

page 50

page 52

Spanish-English Word List

la abeja	the bee
el águila (FEM.)	the eagle
la aguja	the needle
el ala (FEM.)	the wing
el alfiler	the pin
el ananá	the pineapple
el ángel	the angel
el anillo	the ring
el apio	the celery
la araña	the spider
el árbol	the tree
la ardilla	the squirrel
el asno	the donkey
la avispa	the wasp
la bala	the bullet
el brazo	the arm
la bruja	the witch
el buey	the ox
el búfalo	the buffalo
el caballo	the horse
la cabeza	the head
la cadena	the chain
la calabaza	the pumpkin
la calle	the street
la cama	the bed
el camello	the camel
la camisa	the shirt
la campana	the bell
la casa	the house
el castillo	the castle
la cebolla	the onion
el cisne	the swan
la cola	the tail
el corazón	the heart
el cordero	the lamb
la cruz	the cross
el cuaderno	the notebook
la cuchara	the spoon

el cuchillo	the knife
la cuerda	the string
la chaqueta	the jacket
los chiles	the chilis
el dedo	the finger
el diente	the tooth
el elefante	the elephant
el enano	the dwarf
el erizo	the hedgehog
la escuela	the school
la espada	the sword
el espejo	the mirror
la estrella	the star
la falda	the skirt
el gallo	the rooster
el gato	the cat
el gigante	the giant
el globo	the balloon

---

la goma	the eraser
el gusano	the worm
el hacha (FEM.)	the axe
el hada (FEM.)	the fairy
el hamo	the fishhook
el hielo	the ice
la hormiga	the ant
los huevos	the eggs
el iglú	the igloo
la isla	the island
la jarra	the jug
la jaula	the cage
los labios	the lips
el lápiz	the pencil
el lazo	the lasso
el león	the lion
el libro	the book
el lirio	the lily

el lobo — the wolf
el loro — the parrot
la luna — the moon

la llama — the llama
la llave — the key

la mano — the hand
la manzana — the apple
el marco — the frame
la mariposa — the butterfly
el martillo — the hammer
la mesa — the table
el molino — the windmill
el mono — the monkey
el murciélago — the bat

la nariz — the nose
el navío — the warship
el nido — the nest
los niños — the children
la nube — the cloud

el nudo — the knot

el ojo — the eye
las olas — the waves
la olla — the pot
la oreja — the ear
el oso — the bear

el pájaro — the bird
la paloma — the pigeon
la pantera — the panther
el paraguas — the umbrella
el pato — the duck
la pera — the pear
el perro — the dog
el pez — the fish

el pie — the foot
la pierna — the leg
el pino — the pine tree
la pipa — the pipe
el pirata — the pirate

el pozo	the well
el puente	the bridge
la puerta	the door
la pulga	the flea
la rana	the frog
el ratón	the mouse
la red	the net
la reina	the queen
el relámpago	the lightning
el reloj	the watch
el rey	the king
la rodilla	the knee
la rosa	the rose
la sal	the salt
el sapo	the toad
la silla	the chair
la soga	the rope
el sol	the sun
la sombra	the shadow
el sombrero	the hat

la taza	the cup
el techo	the roof
el tenedor	the fork
el tiburón	the shark
la tierra	the earth
el tigre	the tiger
la tinta	the ink
el toro	the bull
el tren	the train
el trigo	the wheat
la uña	the fingernail
la vaca	the cow
el vaso	the drinking glass
la ventana	the window
el vino	the wine
el yate	the yacht
el zapato	the shoe
la zorra	the fox